JOHN WAYNE

JOHN WAYNE

IN THE CAMERA EYE

PHOTOGRAPHY AND COMMENTARY BY **SAM SHAW**

Exeter Books

NEW YORK

Copyright © 1979 by Peebles Press International, Inc.
An Exeter Book
Distributed by Bookthrift, Inc.
New York, New York
ISBN 0-89673-028-X

Entire project supervised by Sam Shaw

Afterword, courtesy of Dore Schary

Design by Jacques Chazaud

Graphic Production by Filmar Graphics, Inc., San Diego, California

Photo Credits
Sam Shaw
Cover, title page, 7, 9-111, 113, 151, back cover
UPI
114-160
Batjac
78, 79, 80 (top), 83

Printed and bound in the United States of America

CONTENTS

1   FOREWORD   7

2   JOHN WAYNE: IN THE CAMERA EYE   9

3   AFTERWORD   111
        by DORE SCHARY

4   JOHN WAYNE: 1907 — 1979   113
        "Let's Move 'Em Out"   115
        The Making of a Legend   116
        The Master and the Disciple   127
        "The Big Trail"   133
        An Extra Star on the American Flag   140
        The Measure of the Man   145

5   THE FILMS OF JOHN WAYNE   151

FOREWORD

When I first began to assemble the photographs of John Wayne for this book, I wasn't conscious of it being a "goodbye" document. But in a way that's what this book is all about.

We had an easy, informal relationship that went back quite a few years. I covered John Wayne for LIFE and LOOK magazines during the filming of "The Alamo" (the first picture the "Duke" directed), and "The Comancheros."

Later, I photographed Wayne at home, in the private world he shared only with his family . . . and in his loneliness, with his hair down.

Within the confines of his home, of himself, this hard-drinking, chain-smoking symbol of the man of action was as gentle as any lover, father and grandfather; as sensitive to writers, artists and photographers of our recent Western past as any historian or poet.

Much has been said about Wayne's Americanism. To me, he was as American as Jane Fonda; as American as Ring Lardner, Sr. and Jr.; as American as John Ford the director, Wayne's idol and guru; as American as John Ford the Leftist politician, who descended from slaves.

This book is a tribute to the screen artist and the man at peak moments in his career. In it, I've tried to capture through pictures and words the legendary figure, the film giant who typified a particular rowdy Hollywood scene from the 1930's through the 1950's . . . the Hollywood of the young John Huston, Bogart and Flynn, which is forever past. And I've also tried to catch the real person behind the celluloid image: the film maker behind the scenes; the cowboy out of the saddle, the grand patriarch on his home grounds.

SAM SHAW

Wayne had many secrets,
many complexities.

Duke Ellington told me,
"A man has four sides."

John Wayne, movie star,
was only one side of him.

...many secrets, many complexities ...

He was always a hard drinking man. He could drink; he was drinking from the beginning.

And smoking continually.

In his early days he'd always get into scrapes. He had a press agent — I met this woman once — whose main job was to keep Wayne out of the papers.

Later, he had a great press agent — Jim Hennigan (who's now living in Spain, writing mystery novels). He was one of the best press agents in Hollywood. A great Irish character. Perhaps the only guy who'd drink Wayne under the table . . . one of the few guys who'd stand up to Wayne. They had a violent friendship in that sense.

One day after a wild drinking spree they found themselves in Acapulco, on a patio in one of their favorite watering holes. In the distance divers were jumping off a 200-foot precipice. Below, tremendous waves smashed against jutting rocks.

Hennigan turned to Wayne and said, "I bet you a round of drinks that I could do that."

Wayne challenged him.

Hennigan went down the steps, behind the cactus, and paid the diver to put on his red trunks.

The young man dove; from a distance you could see only that he was wearing Jim's red trunks.

When the diver came out behind the bushes, Hennigan went into the water, got himself wet, took back his trunks, put them on. Then he came back: everybody applauded.

Jim said, "I did it!"

Wayne said, "You son of a bitch, you really did it! The drinks are on me." And Wayne had to buy drinks for everybody on the patio . . .

If he'd ever found out, I think he'd have beat the crap out of Hennigan.

A genuine man.

Lusty. Hard drinking. Hard smoking. Hard living.

He had everybody's respect . . . He even had the respect of the Left. He might be the only man they'd forgive for defending Nixon.

I don't know if he had affairs with women: being a star, you could knock off a million dames.

I know he was intensely in love with his wives.

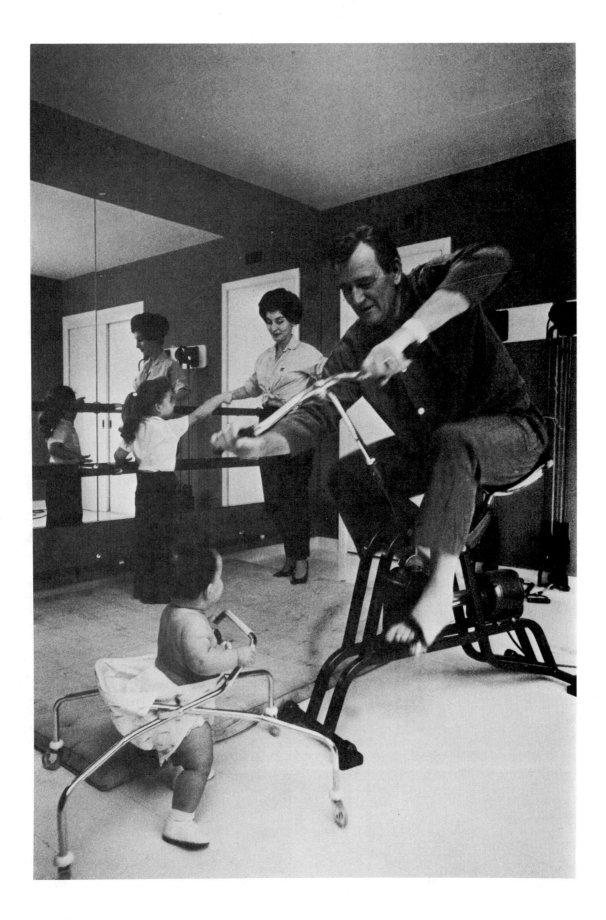

Pilar, Wayne's third wife.

He didn't have time to fool around.

He ran a home.

He ran a business. He actively participated in the business affairs of his company; his son Mike was his producer and business manager.

He also actively participated in the making of pictures. He was always making pictures.

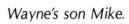
Wayne's son Mike.

Director John Ford (L);
actor Ward Bond (R), a close friend.

Anthony Quinn said:

"Wayne had a reputation as a racist; anti-Mexican, anti-Chicano."

"A racist in speech."

"But he always married a Latin-American, and his kids are part Latin-American. They all come from that background."

His daughter Toni is one of the most beautiful young women I've met.

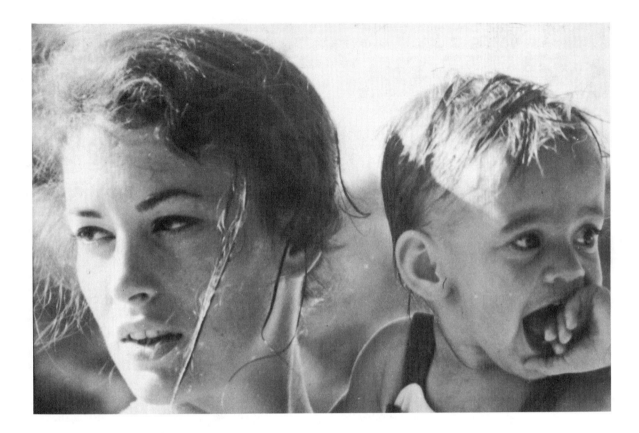

Toni. . .

This is not a detailed rundown of the "Duke's" life, but more my way of showing the bright side of him.

I haven't got all the details of Wayne's life . . .

He loved his sons. He had a lovely relationship with his sons Mike and Pat.

The pictures of them fighting — he was showing how you fight in a movie. How you take a blow. Just horsing around.

Wonderful relationship with his sons and grandchildren. They all liked each other. And respected each other.

Not as a movie star. As a father. As a grandfather.

I've seen families, sons of movie stars, and all that. It's a very difficult life for these youngsters, taking second position to a famous parent. In fact, I think I've seen few instances where it worked well.

John and Gena Cassavettes and their kids. And they work at it; they have to work very hard. They're sensitive to the demands on the kids in the world outside.

The same holds true for Ben Gazzara and Janice Rule . . . And the Peter Falks.

And Wayne. He's the grand master. The great patriarch. In the grand sense; in allowing the children to stand on their own. Even his son Pat — I don't think Wayne ever went out of his way to push Pat into being an actor. The kid would've had to make up his own mind, then he'd back him up. Encourage him.

Showing how you fight in movies; sons Mike (R) and Pat (L).

The guy was a dedicated family man.

You can see by the pictures of his children, his grandchildren.

I like to remember Wayne in his study putting the whole group of kids all around him.

The kids falling around him outside.

The tenderness with his little girl.

That's how the guy was . . . The family was very important.

A dedicated family man. . .

Wayne's study.

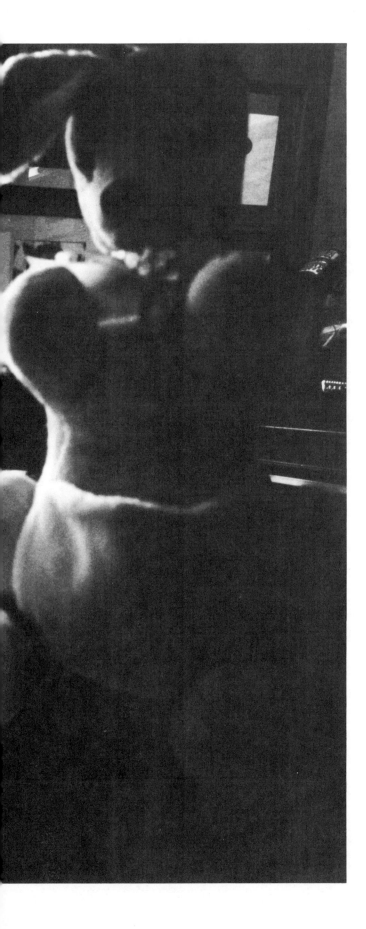

Aissa, Wayne's little girl...

The family was very important...

A gracious host, he ran a gracious house.

Wayne was cultured; very charming, polite, elegant.

Not from what we hear and read about him, but in the confines of his home.

Not even in his friendships with his fellow film makers, but in the confines of himself.

He takes off the toupee in those pictures at home, and there he is with a little bit of hair . . .

The graciousness of that gesture.

In the confines of himself...

at home...
without
toupee...

When Wayne went to Japan with John Huston to make "The Barbarian and the Geisha," he and Huston bought a lot of Japanese art. Wayne bought out the original woodcut blocks from a Buddhist temple. The prints of his wallpaper were made from these woodblocks.

He gave me a print. A beautiful Japanese print. Rice paper. With eight tones of black, and one red.

I've got some of the artifacts in the background of the pictures . . .

Wayne took the western theme very seriously. He had an immense library on the west. He absorbed the west, was steeped in western folklore. He did scholarly studies on the west.

His favorite writer was Emmet Rhodes. I asked him who'd written the best about the west, and he said Rhodes . . .

You know, I'm a professional photographer; and Wayne, an actor, showed me the work of Edward Curtis, an early photographer of American Indians. I only discovered years later that he was one of the greatest photographers. Wayne had a rare portfolio edition, printed by J. P. Morgan, which he bought for $3,000. Bought before Curtis became accepted by the art world. Now it's worth about $500,000, that first edition.

It was Wayne who introduced me to Curtis, a photographer sympathetic to Indians . . .

He was a collector of art objects — his own thing —wherever he went.

But on the set, for the press, he played a guy rolling in the mud.

In the background, some of Wayne's Japanese art.

Wayne had a rough sense of humor. A practical joker,
he was always in on some gag with the guys in the crew.

And pranks; he and those directors all played pranks on
each other . . .

We're out doing "The Alamo" in the boondocks of
Texas; Bracketville. Raw country. Sagebrush country.

Everybody's eating the conventional Hollywood food
that you get on location.

Laurence Harvey was playing an English loner (it was his
first picture in America). Harvey — a very elegant, fancy
living guy, a great gourmet — had his own wines, his
own champagne, his own imported caviar, his own dry
ice containers in the middle of the Texas desert! Shipped
in; so he could eat and drink in this high style at the
commissary tent.

And Wayne loved it!

*Everybody looked at Harvey as an effete English gay
(which Harvey didn't deny — he was double gaited and
made no bones about it).*

*This tough guy Wayne — ordinarily you'd think he'd
make fun of a guy like that too — he just adored Harvey.
Admired him. Had such respect for him (the movie
world knew that Larry Harvey did all his stunts, and
could stand up to the toughest).*

*And Harvey, in the middle of all the tough guys, the
cream of the Hollywood stuntmen, the tempers, the
heat, would go over to Wayne, tweak his cheeks, and
call him "Dukey."*

*No one could tell what might happen. But Wayne would
break up. Then everybody would break up . . .*

*Harvey was quite a character. People would be eating
slop in the heat, and in the middle of everything Harvey
would have his right wine with the right food, his
uniform impeccable.*

Wayne just admired his chutzpah.

*...a laugh
with the guys
on the set...*

James Grant (l.), writer of the screen play for "The Alamo."

Laurence Harvey.

He started out as a member of the crew. He was studying law at U.S.C.

That was Wayne's real ambition — to be a lawyer!

In between classes he worked on the sets as a "go-for."

When he became a superstar, making his own pictures, he used the same crewmen that he himself had worked for as a runner. And he showed them as much respect and subservience while they were working for him as he did when he was a kid. They were father figures to him . . .

In John Ford's presence he was a baby. Ford was Wayne's "Big Daddy."

Ford showed up on the set of "The Alamo" one night, and Wayne turned as obedient as a little boy in front of his master — though he was the producer, director, the star of the film.

Ford walked in on a scene and said, "Your walk there . . ." And he made Wayne go back.

You see, Wayne had walked in his natural manner. But Ford, who had created a rolling gait for him years ago, stopped him and said, "Now you walk like that."

...doing "The Alamo" in the boondocks of Texas...

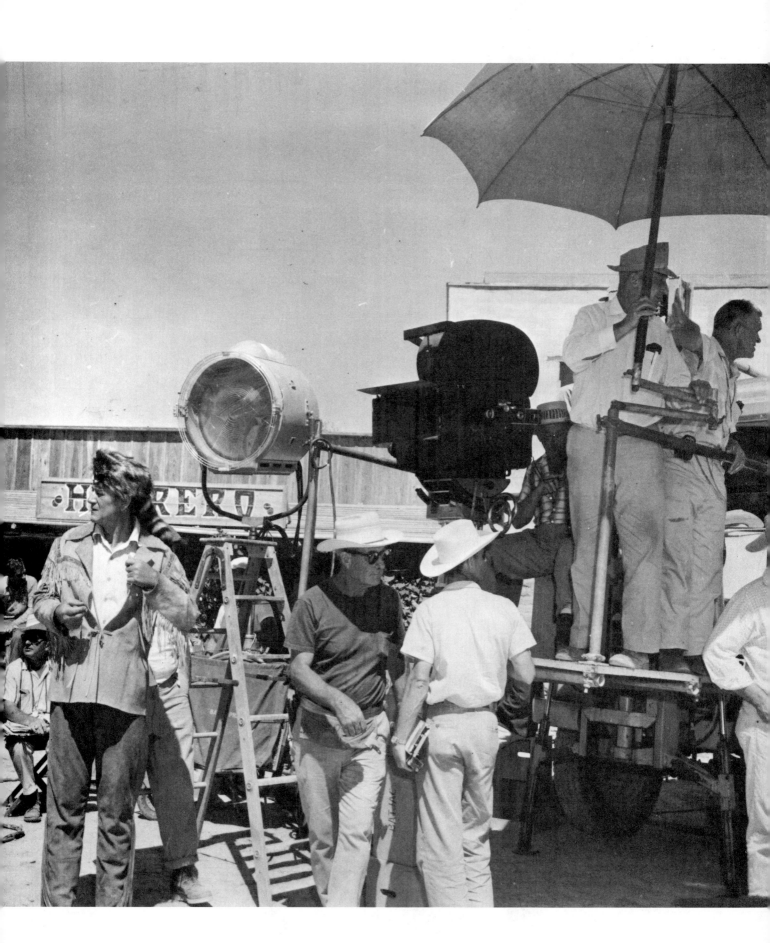

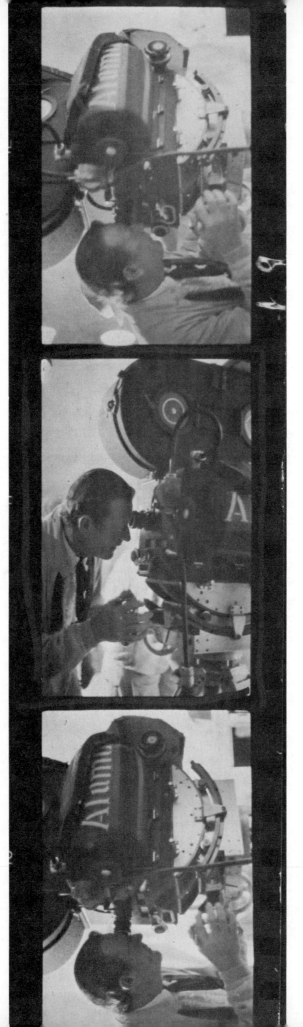

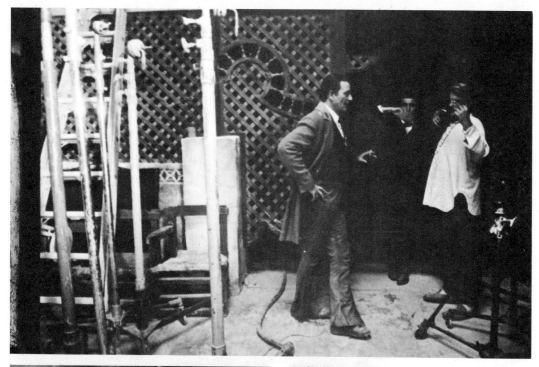

John Ford on the set of "The Alamo."

Wayne as an actor created a certain image. He knew his craft. And he went beyond the stereotype that John Ford created in the beginning.

In "Stagecoach," the image was a masterpiece; the idealization of the cowboy.

When we were kids, reading Zane Grey in The Saturday Evening Post, *seeing Remington's illustrations of the cowboy or Matt Clark's or Harvey Dunn's, Wayne fit that imagery.*

Then he fought to get behind that idealized cowboy, to bring humanism to the celluloid cutouts.

With Richard Widmark (l.)

...a certain image...

Wayne in "The Comancheros."

Bringing humanism to the film image

Wayne's an almost compulsive chess player. He was always playing chess. Between takes he would always play chess. He played with guys in the crew. They were out to lick him; no chess player throws a game.

There was a production manager on a number of
Wayne's pictures, an openly avowed Leftist; and he was
hit by the Red thing. But he was a Communist. Wayne
knew he was a Leftist.

Yet Wayne was very friendly . . . In the middle of all the
Red crap, he gave him a pewter drinking cup, with a
friendly tribute engraved on it . . .

I said to him once, "You're not the reactionary they say
you are."

Wayne replied, "I'm a reactionary?"

I said, "Yes. From where I come, everybody looks upon
you as the leader of the wolf pack."

"Sam," he said, "I'm not the leader of the wolf pack. I'm
not a reactionary."

I replied, "No, you're not. You're a real strong trade
union guy . . . What you are is a Bull Mooser."

He asked, "What's a Bull Mooser?"

"Like Harold Ickes and Theodore Roosevelt," I
answered, "honest, uncorrupted conservatives.
Dedicated American citizens."

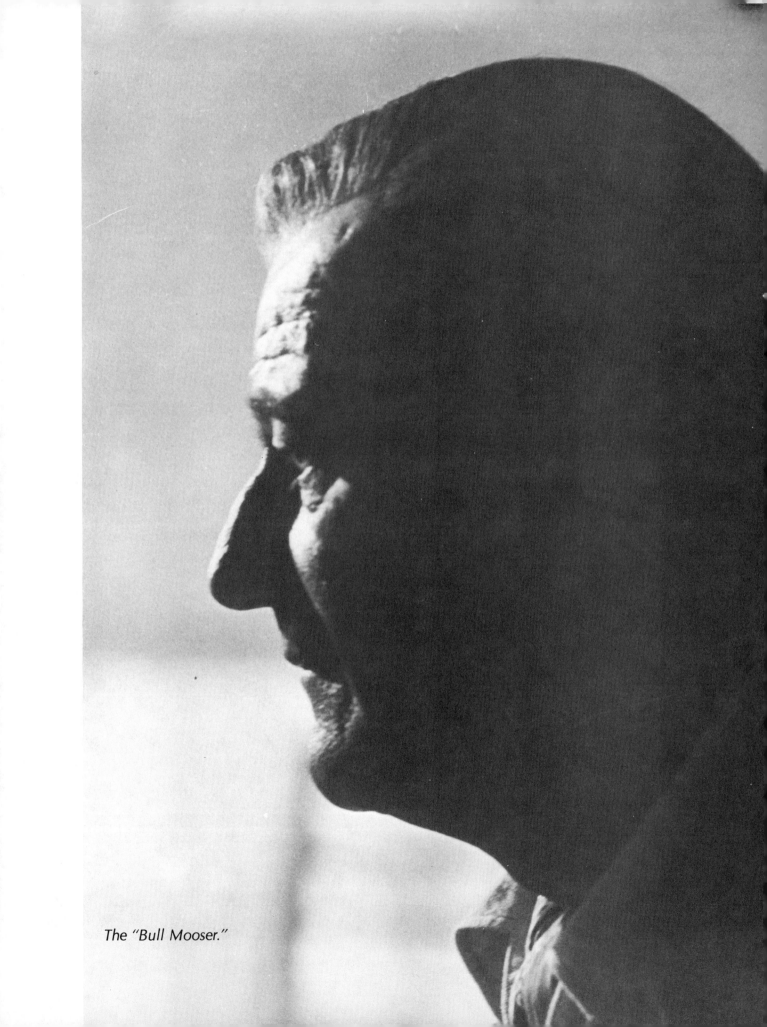

The "Bull Mooser."

3

AFTERWORD

I knew John Wayne, of course, for many years . . .

My first impressions of him were like the first impressions of most people in our business . . . and of American audiences: a sort of apotheosis of the American male, the frontiersman, the one who represented what we thought best in American virtue.

As time went on, I had political differences with Wayne, which were verbal and not really face to face confrontations. They were through things that he said and things that I would write about. I always had a kind of amused attitude about Wayne's politics; and I would really tease him about his politics rather than attack him. I had a feeling that his politics were rather immature — primitive . . .

When he came to Metro (MGM) and did a picture for us (I was then head of production), "The Wings of Eagles", that John Ford directed, I saw John quite frequently . . . Both Johns, as a matter of fact. Our relationships were always very cordial, even though I knew at that time he still had very real concerns about my politics. But I found him an affable and interesting fellow, particularly in the later years.

As his career grew, he mellowed a great deal through the making of some magnificent motion pictures, which will be always a part of the American film heritage . . . some extraordinary movies that will remain as permanent tributes to John.

Even during the times when I found myself in such terrible disagreements with John Wayne's public statements, I would always rush to see his movies because there was something very appealing about them.

And, oddly enough, something that appeared to me to be vulnerable . . . I think that vulnerability was most apparent in the last couple of years of his life, when he was so plagued with his illness.

As we all became very much aware of that vulnerability, we realized that it was combined with a kind of courage that we just, I suppose, automatically expected from him.

So . . . I was saddened by his death . . . And whatever misgivings I sometimes had about my feelings politically about him disappeared a long time ago. They seemed ephemeral, just as I thought they would be . . .

I think that there's not going to be anyone quite like him again.

DORE SCHARY

Wayne's last public appearance, Academy Awards, April '79.

"Let's Move 'Em Out!"

It was a long, long night.

An endless procession of commercials, tired production numbers and tedious acceptance speeches preceded the presentation of the major motion picture awards.

This year there were no streakers, no conspicuous absences, no political filibusters. All in all, the show was professional, sedate and boring. Johnny Carson called it "two hours of sparkling entertainment spread out over four hours."

Finally, the moment arrived that 350 million people had tuned in to watch — the presentation of the Oscar for best picture.

The award itself generated only lukewarm interest. All of the anticipation, all of the excitement, all of the drama of the ceremony was focused on the man who was to present the Oscar: John Wayne.

At 71 years of age, after having survived open heart surgery and two cancer operations, Wayne looked tired and about 40 pounds thinner than usual as he strode briskly to center stage. But his fighting spirit and charismatic personality shone through — the qualities that had made him a leading box office attraction for decades and possibly the best-known American actor in the world.

This, his first public appearance since cancer surgery only three months earlier, sparked an electrical demonstration of respect and affection. The audience rose as one in a standing ovation that went on and on.

As the applause finally subsided, Wayne said, "That's just about the only medicine a fella'd ever really need. Believe me when I tell you I'm mighty pleased that I can amble down here tonight."

What most of the audience didn't realize was that Wayne had undergone a strenuous routine of exercises for at least a week in advance of the Academy Awards ceremony, so he could walk assuredly and stand comfortably before the black-tie crowd.

"Oscar and I have something in common," Wayne continued. "Oscar first came to the Hollywood scene in 1928. So did I. We're both a little weather-beaten, but we're here and plan to be around for a whole lot longer."

There was more applause. It was a moment that brought tears to many eyes around the world.

Then Wayne said, "My job here tonight is to identify your five choices for outstanding picture of the year, and to announce the winner." And in tones he had used at the head of innumerable back-lot cattle drives, he roared, "So let's move 'em out!"

Wayne read the names of the nominees for best film with the strong, drawling voice that has been his trademark in over 200 films, and the award was presented amid thunderous applause. As much as this applause was for the winning movie, it was also for John Wayne, who had played yet another dramatic scene — before one of the largest audiences of his life — with the same rough-hewn dignity that had characterized so many of his performances.

This was his last public appearance.

Less than one month later, Wayne entered the U.C.L.A. Medical Center and had his lower intestine removed. And on June 11, 1979, with his seven children and many of his grandchildren at his bedside, Wayne slipped into a coma and died from complications of cancer.

One of his last requests was for the establishment of a cancer research fund, which the Wayne family announced the day following his death. A family spokesperson requested that those who wished to honor Wayne do so by contributing to the newly established John Wayne Memorial Cancer Fund. Wayne was an "inspiration to other cancer patients around the world," said a spokesperson for the American Cancer Society, because of his honesty and courage in facing the disease.

In Los Angeles, the Olympic Torch atop the Coliseum was lit in the Duke's honor, and flags on all county buildings flew at half mast. Cities across the nation memorialized Wayne by this same poignant act.

John Wayne's continued zest for life delighted not only his directors and co-stars but also the millions of Americans who knew him only as the legendary "Duke."

America loves John Wayne because his legend is our legacy. His fans admired him because he gave them a philosophy they can respect.

Demonstrating the proper way to throw a knife, 1930.

Dressed for role in "The Big Trail" (1930).

The Making of a Legend

When asked to explain John Wayne's enormous popularity, director John Ford — who worked with Wayne on 14 pictures — said, "Duke is the best actor in Hollywood, that's all."

Sometimes it's difficult to remember that Wayne was, after all, an actor. His public image has been so colored by the roles he has played, that the private man has often been overlooked.

One doesn't confuse Laurence Olivier with Hamlet, or Orson Welles with Charles Foster Kane. But somehow it's different with John Wayne. It seems as if Wayne had played himself again and again, in different guises. Or perhaps it was that he internalized his roles.

John Wayne, the man, has been perceived as the embodiment of all the qualities John Wayne, the actor, exhibited in his various movie roles. In fact, General Douglas MacArthur once said that Wayne played the part of "the cavalry officer better than any man who wears a uniform." That's an actor's job, and John Wayne did his job well.

In a very real sense, John Wayne's career as an actor has paralleled the saga of our own national struggle for ideals. His success has been our success. His failures have reflected our own. And he has come to symbolize America as no other personality.

In the beginning, John Wayne's films revealed an actor who had not yet discovered his acting strengths. The roles he played in his early career expose a groping, a searching for a comfortable character.

Wayne once said: "When I started, I knew I was no actor, so I went to work on this Wayne thing. It was as deliberate and studied a projection as you'll ever see. I figured I needed a gimmick, so I dreamed up the drawl, the squint and a way of moving meant to suggest that I wasn't looking for trouble but would just as soon throw a bottle at your head as not. It was hit-or-miss for a while, but it began to develop."

Now, there is no separating the legend from the reality.

* * *

116

Wayne weds Josephine Saenz, his first wife, at the house of Loretta Young (at bride's left), 1933.

The Duke carried his impressive nickname like a title — it fit him snugly. It was an appropriate epithet for the man universally acknowledged as the freelance ambassador of American ideals. (The name "Duke" actually derived from a pet Airedale terrier which Wayne had as a little boy. They were inseparable companions, and soon neighbors and friends were calling the boy by his pet's feisty name — "Duke." "Little Duke," as Wayne was known, kept that name and has even had to tell the story himself when reporters asked whether the name was an allusion to royal connections.)

Duke's roots go back to Winterset, Iowa where his father, Clyde Morrison, was a pharmacist. Clyde and Mary Morrison's first son was born on May 26, 1907, and they gave him an eloquent tongue-twister of a name: Marion Michael Morrison.

When Marion was 5, his father fell into ill-health, and it became necessary for the family to relocate in a more healthful climate. They moved to Palmdale, California, near the Mojave Desert; it was the first sampling of ranch life for the future king of Westerns.

Mr. Morrison's health restored, the family then moved to Glendale, where he opened a drugstore. Duke and his younger brother Bob grew up in this well-known Los Angeles suburb. Wayne admired his father intensely and, among all the advice his father bestowed on him, he recalled in particular three rules of behavior. These were three keys in his father's credo to gentlemanly comportment:

1) Always keep your word;

2) A gentleman never intentionally insults anyone; and

3) Don't go around looking for trouble. But if you ever get into a fight, make sure you win it.

As much as any man can be said to have lived up to his own ethics, Wayne did. Indeed, of all the many words written and spoken about John Wayne, no one ever fails to call him a "gentleman." Actress Colleen Dewhurst, who appeared in two of Wayne's pictures said: "He was very kind and very compassionate . . . I guess he was a gentleman."

* * *

With first wife Josephine, Santa Monica, California, 1933.

Spencer Tracy, Wayne and Wayne's first wife, Josephine, at California desert resort, 1934. Wayne had already gained a reputation as star of "Horse Operas."

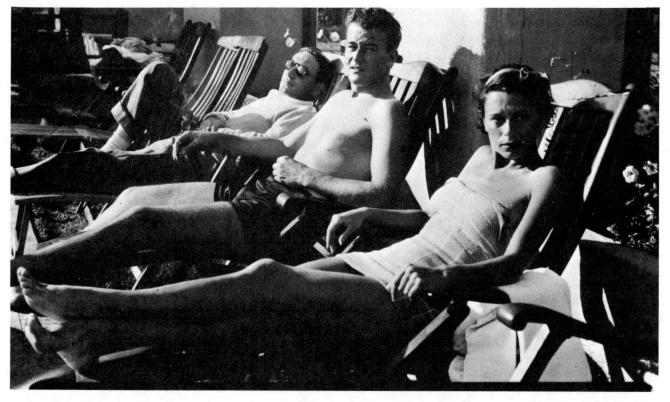

Aboard Wayne's yacht "Venus" with Barbara Read. Los
Angeles Harbor Day, 1937.

Wayne (top, 2nd from rt.) on Hollywood's "All American"
football team, 1934. Fay Wray is team mascot.

Wayne and Claire Trevor in scene from "Stagecoach" (1939).

At Glendale Union High School in California, Duke was an above average student and a top debater. His first love, though, was football. During his junior and senior years, he played on the line and earned a reputation as a hard-hitting tackler. To keep in shape and earn some extra money, he worked on an ice truck hefting 250-pound cakes with old fashioned iron tongs. At various times he also held jobs as a truck driver and fruit picker.

His ambition was to attain an appointment to the Naval Academy at Annapolis, and when that didn't materialize, he was disappointed. His prowess on the gridiron, however, had brought him to the attention of the local scouts from the University of Southern California, and he was awarded an athletic scholarship.

At USC, Wayne was a pre-law student, but football consumed a great deal of his time and energy. He played freshman ball for a year and then was promoted to famed coach Howard Jones' varsity squad. Early in the fall season of his sophomore year, Duke sustained a serious leg injury, which bothered him on and off for the rest of his life. It knocked him off the team, of course, and within a matter of months, Duke withdrew from the university. While on the team, however, Duke spent a lot of time in the movies, thanks to the great matinee cowboy, Tom Mix. Mix was a tremendous fan of USC football. In exchange for 50-yard-line seats at all games, Mix provided Coach Jones' team with movie passes and arranged to get some of the USC players summer jobs at the Fox Studios in Hollywood. Wayne landed a position as "fourth assistant propman" at a salary of $35 a week. His job was to move props and equipment around, and to be a general "go-for." The first picture Duke worked on was "Mother

Wayne autographs Marine PFC Albert Adams' cast at a New
Guinea Hospital station, 1944.

Learning about fighter planes first-hand from Airforce ace
Colonel Neal Kearby in New Guinea during entertainment
tour of Army camps, 1944.

John Wayne and Esperanza Bauer obtain marriage license, Los Angeles, 1946.

"Everybody laughed," Wayne later recalled. The crew, the actors, and most of all Ford. The director then challenged the humiliated youngster to try and tackle him. Ford pretended to be a running player heading for the goal line. He smiled in anticipation of knocking Wayne over a second time.

Wayne leaped forward and kicked the great director good and hard.

Everyone gasped at Wayne's youthful arrogance. But Ford got up laughing. One of the great film friendships of all time was born that day. John Ford had discovered John Wayne. ("I let him have a kick where it would do the most good," Wayne laughed, when telling the story.)

In 1928, Wayne went to work for John Ford. It was also the first time that John Wayne appeared on celluloid. Ford had Wayne working as an extra and as a stuntman. But Ford took time, whenever possible, to show his protégé the ropes. John Ford delighted in sharing his ideas with Wayne. And young John Wayne was learning the movie business — from the master.

Wayne quickly graduated from extra to bit player, from bit player to featured player. Of his first six films, four were made under John Ford's direction.

During the filming of a sequence in John Ford's "Men Without Women," Wayne had the occasion to prove himself to his beloved director. The scene was set in the continually choppy waters of the Pacific off the coast of Catalina Island. The professional stuntmen were not anxious to perform heroic feats in the rough, high waters and Ford called to his fourth assistant property man.

"Show 'em up," he shouted.

Wayne obediently dove into the waves, proving his courage, stunt technique and devotion to Ford all in one shot.

But Wayne had still not discovered his true strength. In his first films — some of the early talkies — he acted as a college football player, an officer in the Navy, a horseplayer; he even sang in a musical!

From 1926 to 1932, Wayne worked in 20 films. His first movies were either directed by John Ford or recommended by Ford. When Raoul Walsh was looking for someone to play the role of Breck Coleman in "The Big Trail," Ford suggested that

Machree," an Irish family saga directed by 31-year-old John Ford, who, incredibly, had already made 55 pictures.

Duke's principal job on "Mother Machree" was to herd a gaggle of geese on and off the set at appropriate times. The first day Ford said not a word to the young man. But on the second day, Ford yelled, "Hey Morrison, aren't you the kid who scored the winning touchdown against Notre Dame last season?" Duke admitted that he was.

"Take your position, will you?" Ford ordered.

Duke obediently hunkered down and got into the set stance, palms on the ground. Ford was a practical joker and a man proud of his own physical condition. Without warning, he lunged at Wayne. The Duke didn't topple easily. But Ford surprised him by kicking one arm out from under him and sent him sprawling on his back.

Wayne might be up to the job. It was Wayne's first lead role — and his first Western.

And it was Walsh who shaped Wayne's "nom de film." Walsh had just finished reading a book about Mad Anthony Wayne, the daring Revolutionary War General, and felt that the name Wayne was rugged and simple. And with John as a first name, it sounded honest — just right for a Western hero.

Wayne went from studio to studio. After two pictures with Fox, he moved to a six-month contract with Columbia. Not all of his pictures were Westerns, and in fact, two of his best films, "The Quiet Man" and "The Long Voyage Home," were of a temperament much different from the wild west films for which he is famed.

Columbia studio head Harry Cohn cast Wayne in such films as "Men Are Like That," in which he played a West Point graduate, and "Maker of Men," in which he was a college football player. He also did a few Westerns for Columbia with time-honored stars such as Buck Jones and Tim McCoy.

Cohn and Wayne locked horns over a love affair with one of Columbia's starlets. Wayne liked her. So did Harry Cohn. As a result, Wayne's contract was not renewed. Typically, John Wayne always refused to reveal her name.

Wayne made only five pictures for Columbia, and when years later Cohn offered Duke roles in big Columbia productions at big salaries, Wayne stalwartly refused. Columbia is the only studio Duke did not work for after he had achieved stardom.

After Columbia, it seemed as if his brief career had ended. In order to eat, Wayne was forced to work in Hollywood's lower depths: the serial films. His first serial was "Shadow of the Eagle." Then he made "The Hurricane Express." If you were to examine his acting in these serials, you would not imagine that this was the same man who won an Oscar for "True Grit." The only thing that shines through in these serials is John Wayne's powerful, unmistakable masculine aura.

But something was happening behind the scenes that was destined to rescue John Wayne from obscurity.

Paramount Pictures discovered that America was on the verge of a love affair with the Western. Every film with Randolph Scott was making money at a phenomenal rate. Fox then got into the business of Westerns, with George O'Brien their stock star.

Meanwhile, Warner was desperately scouting for someone to star in their series of Westerns. Leon Schlesinger, then producer at Warner, was seeking someone who looked like Ken Maynard to re-do the enormously popular Ken Maynard silent Western films.

Schlesinger happened to see one of Wayne's Columbia potboilers. He immediately realized John Wayne had the quality he was seeking. Discovering that Wayne was indeed at liberty, he immediately signed Wayne up for a series of Westerns — as the star.

Schlesinger's insights were right on the mark. Wayne was indeed ready.

Wayne with director Howard Hawks during filming of "Red River" (1948).

In uniform for "Flying Leathernecks" (1951).

The Waynes return from Ireland after John filmed "The Quiet Man," (1951). (l. to r., Michael, Melinda, Patrick, Toni.)

Fans cheer Wayne after settlement of the alimony case brought against him by his second wife, Esperanza Bauer, in 1953.

Embracing Pilar Palette after marriage in Hawaii, 1954, hours after divorce from second wife, Esperanza Bauer, became final.

The Master and the Disciple

John Wayne's film career began in 1928 when director John Ford allowed him to do a "walk-on" in "Mother Machree" (for which he received no screen credit). While continuing work as a propman, Wayne did a bit part in Ford's "Hangman's House," in which he was billed as Michael Morrison.

It was Ford who first realized that this strappingly handsome young man could do more with his brawn than move scenery and more with his talent than play a romantic lead. It was Ford who was able to envision Duke as the lead in "The Big Trail" — not an overly successful film, but a "big movie," and the vehicle which carried Wayne to stardom. It was Ford who knew that Wayne was right for the character of the Ringo Kid in "Stagecoach."

The story goes that Ford asked Wayne to read the script of "Stagecoach" and suggest a suitable actor for the part of the Ringo Kid. Wayne suggested Lloyd Nolan, and Ford considered that for a few moments before exclaiming that it was Wayne he wanted for the Ringo Kid. That movie upgraded the Western from kid stuff to serious cinema.

Between "The Big Trail," released in 1930, and "Stagecoach," released in 1939, Wayne had worked in 57 films co-starring in many of them with people like Laura La Plante, Tim McCoy, Buck Jones, Noah Beery, Barbara Stanwyck, George "Gabby" Hayes, Eleanor Hunt, Ann Rutherford, Jean Rogers, Louise Latimer, Louise Brooks, Alan Ladd and Walter Brennan.

He was paying his dues, a necessary and important part of working his way up the ladder. And over the course of his career, while working on B-Westerns, light comedy or the quality Westerns and war pictures which became his trademark, his friendship with and devotion to John Ford was among the very few constants in his life.

Of Ford, Wayne once said: "I worked on and off for years in menial jobs for him as a prop-boy, stuntman, bit player. I developed a hero worship that still exists. But when I got stuck in three and one-half day Westerns, Ford passed me by without speaking. This went on for three years, he just wouldn't look at me. Then one day, I was at a waterfront bar when Ford's daughter appeared and said, 'Father wants you on his yacht.' I didn't know what to do. Later his wife Mary showed up and said, 'He wants you.'" He finally went to see Ford who revealed that he wanted Wayne to play in "Stagecoach."

"This made me a star," Wayne said, "and I'll be grateful to him forever. But I don't think he ever really had any kind of respect for me as an actor until I made 'Red River' for Howard Hawks ten years later. Even then I was never quite sure."

The team of Ford and Wayne, as director and actor, and as offstage friends, was unbeatable. Ford was a driving director, and when "Stagecoach" came out, the critics agreed that the screen had a bright new star.

Ford directed Wayne in 13 other pictures.

"The Long Voyage Home," ranked one of Duke's very best pictures, was based on plays by Eugene O'Neill.

Boarding Chinese riverboat set in "Blood Alley" (1955).

As Genghis Khan, with Susan Hayward, "The Conqueror" (1956).

Wayne gives Sophia Loren an ungentlemanly boot in the bustle in "Legend of the Lost" (1957).

"They Were Expendable" was a wartime film, starring Robert Montgomery, Donna Reed, and Ward Bond.

"Three Godfathers" was a poignant story of three outlaws who take charge of a newborn baby.

Ford's U.S. Cavalry trilogy, "Fort Apache," "She Wore A Yellow Ribbon" and "Rio Grande" were each extremely successful.

One of Wayne's most memorable and uncharacteristic films, "The Quiet Man," co-starred Maureen O'Hara — who was one of his favorite leading ladies.

"The Searchers" was a heartrending Western with Jeffrey Hunter, Vera Miles, Natalie Wood and Duke's son Pat Wayne, among the stars.

"The Wings of Eagles," the story of an aviator turned playwright, once again coupled Wayne with Maureen O'Hara.

"The Horse Soldiers" was a Civil War story with William Holden and Constance Towers.

Made in 1962, "The Man Who Shot Liberty Valance" was filmed in black and white and showed off John Wayne and Jimmy Stewart at their finest.

"How The West Was Won" became a classic drama of America's westward expansion.

"Donovan's Reef" was the last picture Wayne and Ford made together. Although working for Ford was never an easy task for Wayne, these 14 films represent some of the finest work from the careers of both. Ford believed implicitly in Wayne's talent (especially under his direction), and Wayne's devotion to Ford, whom he alternately called "Pappy" and "The Old Man," knew no bounds. When Duke's son Patrick was born, Ford was asked to be his godfather.

Many years later when Ford was dying of cancer, he called Wayne to visit him at his Palm Springs home. Over a bottle of brandy, the two reminisced and recalled with fondness their friend Ward Bond. After a time Ford wanted to rest, and later that day he died.

Their association spanned more than 30 years — years that saw Michael Morrison grow from a shy but exuberant youth to the stoic John Wayne, a number-one box office attraction for an unprecedented 25 years.

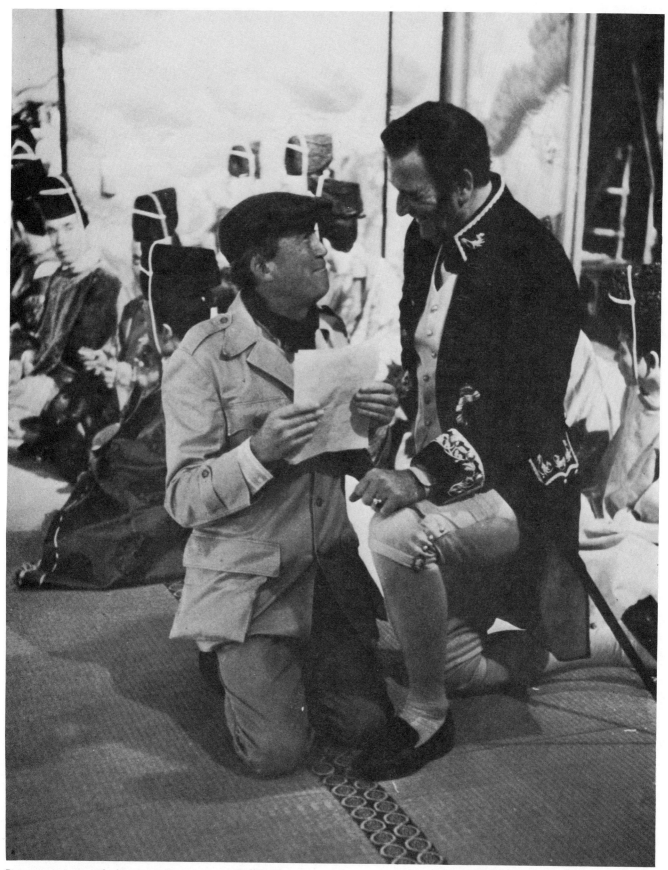

Between scenes with director John Huston in the filming of
"The Barbarian and the Geisha" (1958).

With daughter, Aissa, 2 years old, 1958.

Wayne playing the he-man with Connie Buck (l.) and Nada
Onyx (r.) in "North to Alaska" (1960).

"The Longest Day" (1962).

"The Big Trail"

During the 1930's, Wayne starred in a series of low-budget Westerns. He made a minimum of eight pictures a year for ten years. It has been said that the budgets for these pictures were so low that they could only afford one horse. Yet these smalltime films proved a good training ground for Wayne.

In 1933, after a long courtship, Wayne married Josephine Saenz, a lovely, aristocratic young woman from Panama. They were wed on the patio of actress Loretta Young's Bel Air estate, and they began their life together in a small furnished apartment. The next year their first son Michael was born, followed by daughter Toni in 1936, Patrick in 1937 and Melinda in 1939.

In 1946, after a legal separation which had lasted nearly two years, Wayne and Josephine divorced. That same year he married a young Mexican-born actress, Esperanza Bauer. Their marriage was passionate and tempestuous, but ultimately unhappy, and in 1953 after a highly publicized proceeding, they were divorced. Wayne's third marriage, to Pilar Pallette, a Peru-

vian actress, was a happy one. They had three children, daughter Aissa, son John Ethan, and daughter Marisa Carmela. In 1973 they announced their separation. Wayne has always tried to keep his personal life separate from his career and refused to discuss the reasons for the breakup.

In 1935, Republic Pictures was formed. Its origins were with Mascot Pictures Corporation, for whom Wayne had done several films. Seeking to prove itself as a leading studio, Republic promoted John Wayne's career. He appeared in better films and was loaned to other studios for their films.

It was at this time that he came in contact with stuntman and rodeo rider Yakima Canutt. Wayne credited Canutt for teaching him all the great cowboy stunts he so effectively performed. Among his many talents, Canutt was expert at staging sequences and envisioning the best camera angles to make a stunt seem realistic. This is one of the arts he passed on to Wayne, which Wayne later used in the making of his own productions.

A series of 16 Westerns Wayne made for Monogram pictures starred the Duke in roles of U.S. Marshal, deputy sheriff, undercover agent

Spanking Elizabeth Allen in "Donovan's Reef" (1963).

Doing his own stunts, as usual, 55-year-old Wayne leaps to the ground in "McLintock!" (1963). Maureen O'Hara watches apprehensively.

Wayne tries his hand with a "Bota," or leather wine skin, on location in Spain for "Circus World" (1964).

and all-round "good guy" involved in plots where he either uncovered the bad guys, vindicated a wrongly accused victim, rescued the girl, found a long lost relative or any and all of the aforementioned feats. These pictures were all called Lone Star Westerns, and bore such titles as "Blue Steel," "Lucky Texan," "Texas Terror," and "Rainbow Valley."

While making these Westerns, Wayne and Canutt developed a more dramatic and more realistic style of screen fighting. They created the fast-paced "long punch" and "follow through" still used today. "Yak," Wayne said, "is the best fighter, horse rider and stuntman who ever lived." And he divulged that he borrowed Canutt's "smooth-rolling walk" and soft strong voice. Wayne is also credited with introducing the use of chairs, tables and furniture on hand in barroom brawl scenes. It had previously been taboo for a Western hero to use anything but his fists in a fight.

After continually battling it out in the B-Westerns, Wayne, Ford and "Stagecoach" made it big in 1939. This A-Western established Wayne, and he was able to leave the one-horse pictures behind. His next big film was "The Dark Command" for director Raoul Walsh, co-starring Claire Trevor, Walter Pidgeon, Roy Rogers, George "Gabby" Hayes and Marjorie Main. This was one of the most successful Westerns of the forties and it helped to maintain Wayne's upward climb.

In the 40's, Wayne's reputation as the ideal Western hero began to blossom. He also became the screen's leading war hero, although he made very few important war films.

Wayne was now a major star, and his films continually drew large audiences. He made films with the most successful leading ladies of the day: Marlene Dietrich, Joan Blondell, Anna Lee, Joan Crawford, Jean Arthur, Martha Scott, Donna Reed, Claudette Colbert, Gail Russell, Laraine Day, Shirley Temple, Maureen O'Hara.

During this decade, Wayne's films included seafaring stories, airplane stories, drama, and even comedy, as well as Westerns.

In 1947, Wayne became one of the first major actors to produce films. "Angel and the Badman," his first production, was a well-received Western starring Gail Russell, Bruce Cabot and Harry Carey, Sr. His second production, "The Fighting Kentuckian," was not as successful, but is noteworthy for its use of the comedic talents of Oliver Hardy (minus partner Stan Laurel).

It was at this point in his career that John Wayne became, at the age of 40, the number-one box-office draw. Wayne films played simultaneously in theatres; new releases sharing the bill with re-releases of his earlier films. He remained among the top 10 screen stars for an unprecedented 25 years.

At the close of the 40's, Wayne found himself to be an established star who could exercise more selectivity in accepting and shaping roles, as well as a new producer who would have an input

On set of "El Dorado" (1967), showing son John Ethan how to handle a gun.

in determining what type of pictures would be presented.

The most impressive role Wayne played in the 1950's was that of Sean Thornton in "The Quiet Man." He also made three films for Howard Hughes. The first, "Jet Pilot," was completed in 1950, but was not released until 1957. The second, "Flying Leathernecks," released in 1951, was an action-packed war story co-starring Robert Ryan. The third, "The Conqueror," has been called one of Wayne's worst films.

In 1954, Wayne re-formed his production company and named it Batjac. Today his son Michael is in charge of the company. One of Batjac's first pictures was "Blood Alley" teaming Wayne and Lauren Bacall — a vital pair on screen.

During the 50's, Wayne strayed from the Western a bit more than his public wanted him to, yet throughout the decade he maintained his position among the top 10 box-office attractions.

In 1960, John Wayne realized a dream. For years he had wanted to recreate the battle of the Alamo in an historically accurate film with all the passion and in vivid detail.

"The Alamo," produced by, directed by and starring John Wayne, was a $12 million project; unfortunately, it was not successful. Wayne openly admitted that because the film had lost so much money, he was on the edge of bankruptcy. He then plunged himself into a series of films —mainly the ever-popular John Wayne Westerns. In the next four years he made nine films.

Suddenly, in 1964, John Wayne discovered he had cancer. Surgeons removed a major portion of one lung, and he returned to his career.

At first, his publicity agents did not want the news of Wayne's illness released. They felt it would destroy his hero's image. But Wayne rightly felt that his speaking to the public about how he admitted, faced and dealt with the disease could benefit hundreds of other people. He went on record urging people to seek checkups and pointing out how early detection can save lives. His efforts, as a major personality, in speaking up about cancer, were immeasurable.

After Wayne had "licked the Big C," as he called it, he returned to his work. Once again he was the indomitable cowboy in films like "The

Sons of Katie Elder," "War Wagon," "El Dorado," and his crowning glory, "True Grit." For this last film, Wayne — after more than 40 years in film —received the coveted Oscar for Best Actor.

The very day after winning the Oscar, Wayne returned to the set of "Rio Lobo," the film he was then making, and found the cast, crew and even his horse, Dollar, wearing eye-patches like the one Rooster Cogburn wore in "True Grit."

Wayne was now over 60 years old and had no intention of retiring. He followed "True Grit" with "The Undefeated" (also in 1969), "Chisum" and "Rio Lobo" in 1970; "Big Jake" in 1971; "The Cowboys" in 1972; "The Train Robbers" and "Cahill" in 1973; "McQ" in 1974; "Rooster Cogburn," which co-starred Katharine Hepburn in her first Western, in 1975; and "The Shootist" in 1976.

In his last picture, "The Shootist," Wayne portrayed an aged gunslinger who discovers he has "a cancer" and little time left to live.

Wayne's grandson, Matthew Munos (from daughter Toni) visits him on set of "El Dorado" (1967).

Taking rifle practice on set of "The Sons of Katie Elder" (1965).

Howard Keel, playing an Indian, slugs Wayne to begin a bar room brawl in "The War Wagon" (1967).

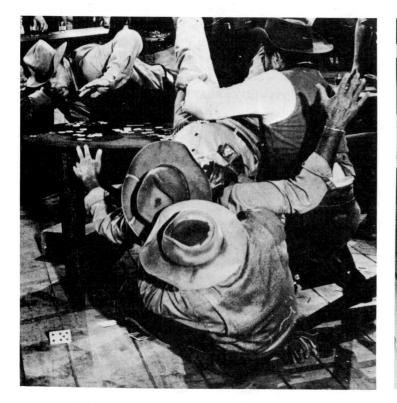

Brawl over, Wayne looks pleased. "The War Wagon" (1967).

With Robert Mitchum in "El Dorado" (1967).

An Extra Star on the American Flag

The characters John Wayne played were always larger than life. Some were on the wrong side of the law. Still, there was something inherently decent about all of the men he portrayed. They were loyal to a personal code — even if they didn't do everything "by the book."

Wayne once put it this way: "I've had one rule that I've tried to make sure came through in every picture, and that was that I played parts men could identify with. Although my characters might do cruel or rough things, they were never mean or petty, never small. That has probably come through because that is my feeling toward life. I have just not accepted any parts that were not that way."

Wayne frequently turned down offers to play weak or flawed characters in major films. The virtues he respected in a man were the virtues he sought in a part: clear-cut attitudes, gallantry toward women, a willingness to fight for what one believes in, self-reliance, honor, instinctive generosity that stops short of charity, and an unabashed love of country. More than any other actor, he insisted on modifying his parts to suit his own ideals and attitudes.

Indeed, it is striking to realize the extent to which his screen persona and personal views coincided. In a 1971 interview with *Playboy*, for instance, he declared that among the greatest pleasures in life were "a good horse under you" and "the sound of a kid calling you Dad for the first time."

"I always look for a story with basic emotions," he once told reporters. "A dog, a kid, a woman's love, a man's love." All of his roles, even in bad movies (and he once admitted, "I've been in more bad pictures than just about anyone in the business"), had a genuine humanity about them. And it has been this quality, more than any other, which explains his appeal to so many different kinds of audiences.

The French director Jean-Luc Godard said that Wayne's humanity is so evident that it can overcome a moviegoer's prejudices against Wayne's outspoken political positions. "I hate John Wayne [for] upholding Goldwater and love him tenderly when abruptly he takes Natalie Wood into his arms in the next-to-last reel of 'The Searchers.'"

"I'm proud of every day in my life I wake up in the United States of America," Wayne once said. Not in a movie — but in an address to a Republican National Convention. His patriotism was so genuine and fervent that a writer once described him as "an extra star on the American flag."

President Carter eulogized Wayne as "a symbol of many of the most basic qualities that made America great. [His] ruggedness, tough independence, sense of personal conviction and courage — on and off screen — reflected the best of our national character."

Indeed his personal character and that of our nation have become emotionally and emblematically entwined.

In what was probably the most controversial production of Wayne's career, his 1968 war story "The Green Berets," he gave vent to his staunchly patriotic views on the Vietnam war. Wayne co-directed the film, which was produced by Batjac and released by Warners-Seven Arts. He received a tremendous amount of criticism for this film. His unquestioning patriotism was becoming less and less popular as the Vietnam war grew to be a rallying point of the 60's. Wayne's glorification of soldiers' technique, particularly in this war, incensed many and pleased few. Nevertheless — it was one of a very few films made during the war which focused on the war. And despite, or perhaps because of, the controversy it made a profit.

The film depicted the Vietnam conflict as a clear-cut example of altruism — America rushing in to save a small nation from outside, Communist attackers. While this had been the popular belief during previous years, in 1968, when the film was released, America had come almost completely to feel that that opinion had been a naive conception of the situation. John Wayne's views, synonymous with conservative America, were waning in their popularity, and he appeared, even more so, as a bastion of vanishing American idealism.

In May of 1979, Elizabeth Taylor and Maureen O'Hara appeared before a Congressional committee pressing for the forging of a commemorative medal in honor of John Wayne. On June 12, just one day after the actor's death, the Mint announced that it would accept mail orders for a bronze medal inscribed "John Wayne, American."

Playing chess with James Caan on set of "El Dorado" (1967).

Directing a scene from "The Green Berets" (1968).

Accepting "Oscar" in 1970 for his performance in "True Grit".

Wayne and Rock Hudson on the trail in "The Undefeated" (1970).

Celebrating Wayne's "Oscar" for "True Grit", entire cast of
"Rio Lobo" (1970) dons eye-patches. Director Howard Hawks
to Wayne's left.

On location for "Rio Lobo" (1970).

The Measure of the Man

In his almost 50-year film career, John Wayne played many roles — all of them exciting, boldly adventurous, larger than life. Many of these characters have become household words. His portrayal of these characters is what won John Wayne the tremendous following he has. John Wayne must be considered one of America's strongest screen personalities. Here are just a few of the outstanding characters Wayne played:

Breck Coleman in "The Big Trail" — This portrayal of a wagon train leader who avenges the murder of his friend was directed by Raoul Walsh.

Peter Brooks in "Girls Demand Excitement" — Wayne played a down-and-out college student working his way through college. In a war between the boys and the girls, Wayne is the leader of the boys.

Gordon Wales in "Three Girls Lost" — Wayne is an architect wrongfully accused of murdering a neighbor.

Lt. Bob Denton in "Men Are Like That" — Wayne plays a West Point cadet and football player who finds his former girlfriend married to his new commanding officer.

Clint Turner in "Range Feud" — Wayne is the son of a rancher who is accused of murdering his father's rival. He is later saved by the sheriff who finds the real culprit.

Buzz Kinney in "Lady and Gent" — Wayne plays an up-and-coming young boxer who knocks down a veteran prizefighter — and later receives a beating himself.

Craig McCoy in "Shadow of the Eagle" — Wayne is a pilot employed by a fairground operator who pursues a villain who calls himself "The Eagle."

Larry Baker in "The Hurricane Express" — In this railroad story, Wayne plays the son of a man murdered by a villain called "The Wrecker." Wayne seeks to avenge his father's death by finding the murderer's true identity.

Tom Wayne in "The Three Musketeers" — Wayne is the brave soldier who rescues three French Legionnaires held by rebels in the Arabian desert.

Dick Wallace in "His Private Secretary" — Wayne, the son of a wealthy businessman, can't concentrate on business because he's so taken with women. He eventually meets the female who straightens him out.

In his early years, as you can see from the roles mentioned above, Wayne attempted to portray every type of character that came his way. It was the best education for the man who was to become one of America's most beloved actors. He also worked with some of the top directors in Hollywood.

In the dozen or so films that followed, Wayne discovered his greatest power — the ability to play in Westerns as both hero and villain. It was the beginning of a love affair between Wayne and the American public.

John Drury in "Ride Him, Cowboy" — Wayne, a cowboy who tracks down the murderer of a rancher, trains a horse named "Duke" to find the killer.

John Steele in "The Big Stampede" — Wayne is a deputy sheriff who tracks down a local rancher accused of killing several officers of the law.

On location for "Rio Lobo" (1970). Young Chris Mitchum ponders Wayne's next chess move.

John Holmes in "The Man From Monterey" — Wayne as an Army Captain keeps an elderly Spanish man from losing his land, uncovers fraud and saves the girl from a bad marriage.

Jimmy McCoy in "Baby Face" — Wayne plays a bit part as assistant manager of a bank who helps his friend to the top and is later deserted by her.

Sandy Saunders in "Riders of Destiny" — Wayne plays an undercover government agent who exposes a villain's control of ranchers' water supply.

John Brant in "Sagebrush Trail" — Wayne, a cowboy wrongly charged with murder, escapes prison in search of the real killer. He joins a gang and befriends the real murderer, who ends up losing his life.

Jerry Mason in "The Lucky Texan" — Wayne, as a recent college graduate, joins his late father's partner in a search for gold and fights off usurpers. In the process, Wayne is blamed for robbery and murder, but discovers the guilty party.

Ted Hayden in "West of the Divide" — Wayne plays a pseudo-outlaw who confronts and fights his father's murderer.

Ringo Kid in "Stagecoach" — Wayne as an escaped jailbird who seeks the killers of his father and brother, fights off the Indians and treats a prostitute like a lady, while riding in the Stagecoach.

Bob Seton in "The Dark Command" — Wayne plays a pre-Civil War cowboy who gets elected town marshal. The man who lost that election plots against Wayne, his wife, brother-in-law, and eventually the town itself.

John Mason in "Haunted Gold" — Wayne plays a man who searches for an abandoned gold mine in a ghost town and runs into a den of thieves.

John Trent in "The Telegraph Trail" — Wayne, an Army scout, leads an expedition of men and supplies to the camp of the men who are stringing the first telegraph wire across the western plains.

John Bishop in "Somewhere in Sonora" — Wayne as a cowboy accused of improprieties during a rodeo, reinstates himself in everyone's good graces after he foils a plot to rob a silver mine and recovers his boss's missing son.

John Phillips in "Three Faces West" —Wayne is a dust-bowl farmer who befriends a Viennese surgeon and falls in love with his daughter. Both have escaped concentration camps and wish to settle in the Mid-West. The dust bowl rages and Wayne leads a party to Oregon.

In John Wayne's "second period," he acted primarily in Westerns. Wayne played every type of character — "good guys" and "bad guys." In all of these roles, John Wayne brought a strength to the screen, an ability to command the audience. No matter what role he played, John Wayne was always a dominant character. Few actors have remained at the top for so long a period of time, and few actors have survived so many truly bad films with their reputations intact. John Wayne was still learning. During this time he was learning that the public liked him most as a hero — the good guy who believed right must win over wrong.

Jack Stuart in "Reap the Wild Wind" — Wayne plays a steamship captain of the 1840's whose first boat is run aground by pirates. Taking unauthorized command of a second boat, he is charged with sabotage but dies in an underwater examination of the wreckage.

Roy Glennister in "The Spoilers" — Wayne plays an Alaskan miner who has to fight a corrupt lawyer and commissioner to retain his rightful claim.

Tom Craig in "In Old California" —Wayne is a Sacramento pharmacist who fights a local political boss and wins his fiancee.

Jim Gordon in "Flying Tigers" — Wayne is the commanding officer of a regiment of American fliers fighting the Japanese.

Duke Hudkins in "Lady Takes a Chance" — Wayne plays a rodeo rider who beats Jean Arthur's three suitors to win her hand in marriage.

Rocklin in "Tall in the Saddle" — Wayne is a cowboy who tries to help a lady win her rightful inheritance and discovers he is the nephew of a ranch owner.

Rusty Ryan in "They Were Expendable" — Wayne plays a Navy Lieutenant in the Pacific during World War II.

Disciple and master: Wayne and John Ford shortly before Ford's death in 1973.

Down the rapids with Katherine Hepburn in "Rooster Cogburn" (1975).

John Devlin in "Dakota" — Wayne plays an ex-soldier turned farmer who contends against two swindlers while his wife plots against her corrupt father.

Quirt Evans in "Angel and the Badman" — Wayne plays an injured gunfighter taken in by a Quaker. By the end of the film, Wayne has reformed and no longer needs his gun.

Kirby York in "Fort Apache" — Wayne plays a U.S. Cavalry Captain whose easygoing command of a fort is cut short by the arrival of the new hard-line commanding colonel (played by Henry Fonda).

Thomas Dunson in "Red River" — Wayne is a post-Civil War Texas cattleman who leaves the impoverished South to begin the first Missouri-bound cattle drive over the now famous Chisholm Trail.

Captain Ralls in "Wake of the Red Witch" — Wayne plays the captain of a ship owned by his greedy rival-in-love's trading empire.

Nathan Brittles in "She Wore A Yellow Ribbon" — Wayne plays an aging Army Captain who refuses to accept his inevitable retirement. His warm humanity combined with sternness makes this one of Wayne's best roles.

During the "third period" of John Wayne's acting career, he consistently played men of strength, power, principles and ideals. It was a role he became easily accustomed to because it was the role he played in life.

Sean Thornton in "The Quiet Man" — Wayne plays a boxer who, after a death in the ring, returns to Ireland and the cottage in which he was born, asking nothing more than peace. His troubles have just begun.

Jim McLain in "Big Jim McLain" — Wayne plays a special agent sent to Hawaii to investigate a terrorist ring.

Steve Williams in "Trouble Along the Way" — Wayne plays a football coach fighting for custody of his young daughter.

Captain Dooley in "Island in the Sky" — Wayne as the pilot of a crashed transport plane, keeps his crew in good spirits as they wait to be rescued.

Hondo Lane in "Hondo" — Wayne plays an ex-gunfighter and cavalry scout who protects a woman and her young son, and later unwittingly kills the woman's runaway husband.

Dan Roman in "The High and the Mighty" — Wayne plays a commercial airline co-pilot who takes over to prevent a crash and then encourages the pilot to guide the plane to a safe landing.

Ethan Edwards in "The Searchers" — Wayne plays an Old West fighter who becomes obsessed with avenging his brother's death and finding his two nieces.

Townsend Harris in "The Barbarian and the Geisha" — Wayne is the first American ambassador to Japan.

John T. Chance in "Rio Bravo" — Wayne plays the sheriff who must save his community from a band of outlaws.

With James Stewart between scenes during the filming of "The Shootist" (1976).

John Marlowe in "The Horse Soldiers" — Wayne is a Union Colonel in the Civil War who leads a regiment on a mission to destroy a Confederate railroad.

Davy Crockett in "The Alamo" — Wayne plays the legendary hero defending the Alamo. Wayne also produced and directed this film which was the realization of a dream for him.

Jake Cutter in "The Comancheros" — Wayne is a Texas Ranger Captain who outwits the Comancheros, a ruthless group of outlaws.

Tom Doniphon in "The Man Who Shot Liberty Valance" — Wayne is a Western gunfighter who protects lawyer/politician Ranse Stoddard (James Stewart) from outlaw Liberty Valance (Lee Marvin).

Benjamin Vandervoort in "The Longest Day" — Wayne plays an Allied officer during D-Day, World War II.

William T. Sherman in "How the West Was Won" — Wayne plays the famous Union General in the Civil War scenes of this movie.

George Washington McLintock in "McLintock" — Wayne plays a mine owner, timber baron, cattle king and empire builder who has the whole town eating out of his hand.

Centurion in "The Greatest Story Ever Told" — Wayne plays a Roman soldier who witnesses Jesus' crucifixion.

Rockwell Torey in "In Harm's Way" — Wayne plays a Navy Captain in the Pacific in World War II, a captain more inclined to follow himself than to obey orders.

John Elder in "The Sons of Katie Elder" — Wayne is the oldest son of a family bent on investigating their father's mysterious death.

Cole Thornton in "El Dorado" — Wayne plays a wandering gunfighter whose worst enemy is his own declining ability to fight.

Mike Kirby in "The Green Berets" — Wayne is a Vietnam War Colonel in command of a specialized group of fighters.

The American film was maturing as was John Wayne himself. In the next phase of his films, we see a man who is more content with life, more understanding, more resigned to the fates — whatever they may be. John Wayne's character on screen, though, didn't alter. His roles remained strong, yet they were always tinged with a certain honesty that seemed to come with age.

Rooster Cogburn in "True Grit" — Wayne plays a gruff one-eyed deputy U.S. Marshal who catches the murderer of young Mattie Ross' (Kim Darby) father. That won him the Academy Award as Best Actor in 1969.

Cord McNally in "Rio Lobo" — Wayne is a former Union Army Captain seeking revenge on a traitor who led Confederates to a gold shipment.

Jake McCandles in "Big Jake" — Wayne is the virtual owner of a town, who comes back to his ranch and family after his grandson is kidnapped.

Wil Peterson in "The Cowboys" — Wayne as a 60-year-old rancher who leads a group of young kids in a cattle drive after his regular hired hands run off to find gold.

Lon McQ in "McQ" — As a police lieutenant, Wayne investigates the murder of a fellow officer and winds up exposing police corruption.

Although John Wayne's many roles were widely varied, the characters he played were always strong, decisive, and compelling — very much like the man himself.

5

"The Big Trail" (1930).

The Films of John Wayne

THE DROP KICK 1927 (Warner Brothers). The cast included Richard Barthelmess, Barbara Kent, Hedda Hopper and Dorothy Revier. Director was Millard Webb.

MOTHER MACHREE 1928 (Twentieth Century-Fox). The cast included Neil Hamilton, Victor McLaglen and Ted McNamara. Director was John Ford.

HANGMAN'S HOUSE 1928 (Twentieth Century-Fox). The cast included Victor McLaglen, June Collyer, Larry Kent and Earle Foxe. Director was John Ford.

SALUTE 1929 (Twentieth Century-Fox). The cast included George O'Brien, Helen Chandler, Stepin Fetchit and Frank Albertson. Directors were John Ford and David Butler.

WORDS AND MUSIC 1929 (Twentieth Century-Fox). The cast included Lois Moran, David Percy and William Orlamond. Director was James Tinling.

MEN WITHOUT WOMEN 1930 (Twentieth Century-Fox). The cast included Kenneth MacKenna, Frank Albertson and Paul Page. Director was John Ford.

ROUGH ROMANCE 1930 (Twentieth Century-Fox). The cast included George O'Brien, Helen Chandler and Antonio Moreno. Director was A. F. Erickson.

CHEER UP AND SMILE 1930 (Twentieth Century-Fox). The cast included Arthur Lake, Dixie Lee and Olga Baclanova. Director was Sidney Lanfield.

THE BIG TRAIL 1930 (Twentieth Century-Fox). The cast included Marguerite Churchill, Tully Marshall, Tyrone Power, Sr., and Ward Bond. Director was Raoul Walsh.

GIRLS DEMAND EXCITEMENT 1931 (Twentieth Century-Fox). The cast included Virginia Cherrill, Marguerite Churchill and William Janney. Director was Seymour Felix.

THREE GIRLS LOST 1931 (Twentieth Century-Fox). The cast included Loretta Young, Lew Cody and Joan Marsh. Director was Sidney Lanfield.

MEN ARE LIKE THAT 1931 (Columbia). The cast included Laura La Plante, June Clyde and Forrest Stanley. Director was George B. Seitz.

RANGE FEUD 1931 (Columbia). The cast included Buck Jones, Susan Fleming, Ed LeSaint and Harry Woods. Director was D. Ross Lederman.

MAKER OF MEN 1931 (Columbia). The cast included Jack Holt, Richard Cromwell, Joan Marsh and Robert Allen. Director was Edward Sedgwick.

HAUNTED GOLD 1932 (Warner Brothers). The cast included Sheila Terry, Harry Woods, Erville Alderson and Otto Hoffman. Director was Mack V. Wright.

SHADOW OF THE EAGLE 1932 (Mascot). The cast included Dorothy Gulliver, Richard Tucker, Lloyd Whitlock and Walter Miller. Director was Ford Beebe.

HURRICANE EXPRESS 1932 (Mascot). The cast included Shirley Grey, Tully Marshall, Conway Tearle and J. Farrell MacDonald. Directors were Armand Schaefer and J. P. McGowan.

TEXAS CYCLONE 1932 (Columbia). The cast included Tim McCoy, Shirley Grey and Wallace MacDonald. Director was D. Ross Lederman.

LADY AND GENT 1932 (Paramount). The cast included George Bancroft, Charles Starrett and James Gleason. Director was Stephen Roberts.

TWO-FISTED LAW 1932 (Columbia). The cast included Walter Brennan, Tully Marshall and Alice Day. Director was D. Ross Lederman.

RIDE HIM, COWBOY 1932 (Warner Brothers). The cast included Ruth Hall, Harry Gribbon and Frank Hagney. Director was Fred Allen.

THE BIG STAMPEDE 1932 (Warner Brothers). The cast included Noah Beery, Mae Madison and Berton Churchill. Director was Tenny Wright.

THE TELEGRAPH TRAIL 1933 (Warner Brothers). The cast included Marceline Day, Otis Harlan and Yakima Canutt. Director was Tenny Wright.

CENTRAL AIRPORT 1933 (Warner Brothers). The cast included Richard Barthelmess, Sally Eilers and Tom Brown. Director was William A. Wellman.

HIS PRIVATE SECRETARY 1933 (Showmen's Pictures). The cast included Evalyn Knapp, Natalie Kingston and Arthur Hoyt. Director was Philip A. Whitman.

SOMEWHERE IN SONORA 1933 (Warner Brothers). The cast included Shirley Palmer, Henry B. Walthall and Paul Fix. Director was Mack V. Wright.

THE LIFE OF JIMMY DOLAN 1933 (Warner Brothers). The cast included Douglas Fairbanks, Jr. and Loretta Young. Director was Archie Mayo.

THE THREE MUSKETEERS 1933 (Mascot). The cast included Ruth Hall, Noah Beery, Jr. and Jack Mulhall. Director was Armand Schaefer.

BABY FACE 1933 (Warner Brothers). The cast included Barbara Stanwyck, George Brent and Donald Cook. Director was Alfred E. Green.

THE MAN FROM MONTEREY 1933 (Warner Brothers). The cast included Ruth Hall, Nena Quartero, Luis Alberni and Francis Ford. Director was Mack V. Wright.

RIDERS OF DESTINY 1933 (Monogram). The cast included Cecilia Parker, George Hayes and Forrest Taylor. Director was Robert N. Bradbury.

SAGEBRUSH TRAIL 1933 (Monogram). The cast included Lane Chandler, Yakima Canutt, Wally Wales and Art Mix. Director was Armand Schaefer.

COLLEGE COACH 1933 (Warner Brothers). The cast included Dick Powell, Pat O'Brien and Ann Dvorak. Director was William A. Wellman.

LUCKY TEXAN 1934 (Monogram). The cast included Barbara Sheldon, George Hayes, Lloyd Whitlock and Yakima Canutt. Director was Robert N. Bradbury.

WEST OF THE DIVIDE 1934 (Monogram). The cast included Virginia Brown Faire, Lloyd Whitlock and Yakima Canutt. Director was Robert N. Bradbury.

BLUE STEEL 1934 (Monogram). The cast included Eleanor Hunt, George Hayes and Yakima Canutt. Director was Robert N. Bradbury.

THE MAN FROM UTAH 1934 (Monogram). The cast included Polly Ann Young, George Hayes and Yakima Canutt. Director was Robert N. Bradbury.

RANDY RIDES ALONE 1934 (Monogram). The cast included George Hayes, Alberta Vaughn and Yakima Canutt. Director was Harry Fraser.

THE STAR PACKER 1934 (Monogram). The cast included Verna Hillie, George Hayes, Yakima Canutt and Earl Dwire. Director was Robert N. Bradbury.

THE TRAIL BEYOND 1934 (Monogram). The cast included Verna Hillie, Noah Beery and Noah Beery, Jr. Director was Robert N. Bradbury.

NEATH ARIZONA SKIES 1934 (Monogram). The cast included Sheila Terry, Jay Wilsey, Yakima Canutt and Jack Rockwell. Director was Harry Fraser.

LAWLESS FRONTIER 1935 (Monogram). The cast included Sheila Terry, George Hayes, Earl Dwire and Yakima Canutt. Director was Robert N. Bradbury.

Wayne finishes off Jack Clifford in a scene from a 1936 "Horse Opera."

TEXAS TERROR 1935 (Monogram). The cast included LeRoy Mason, George Hayes, Buffalo Bill, Jr. and Bert Dillard. Director was Robert N. Bradbury.

RAINBOW VALLEY 1935 (Monogram). The cast included Lucille Browne, LeRoy Mason, George Hayes and Bert Dillard. Director was Robert N. Bradbury.

PARADISE CANYON 1935 (Monogram). The cast included Marion Burns, Yakima Canutt, Reed Howes and Perry Murdock. Director was Carl Pierson.

THE DAWN RIDER 1935 (Monogram). The cast included Marion Burns, Yakima Canutt, Reed Howes and Denny Meadows. Director was Robert N. Bradbury.

WESTWARD HO 1935 (Republic). The cast included Sheila Mannors, Frank McGlynn, Jr., Jack Curtis and Yakima Canutt. Director was Robert N. Bradbury.

DESERT TRAIL 1935 (Monogram). The cast included Mary Kornman, Paul Fix, Edward Chandler and Lafe McKee. Director was Collin Lewis.

NEW FRONTIER 1935 (Republic). The cast included Muriel Evans, Mary McLaren, Warner Richmond and Sam Flint. Director was Carl Pierson.

LAWLESS RANGE 1935 (Republic). The cast included Sheila Mannors, Earl Dwire, Jack Curtis and Yakima Canutt. Director was Robert N. Bradbury.

THE LAWLESS NINETIES 1936 (Republic). The cast included Ann Rutherford, Lane Chandler, Harry Woods and George Hayes. Director was Joseph Kane.

KING OF THE PECOS 1936 (Republic). The cast included Muriel Evans, Cy Kendall, Jack Clifford and Yakima Canutt. Director was Joseph Kane.

THE OREGON TRAIL 1936 (Republic). The cast included Ann Rutherford, Yakima Canutt, Frank Rice and Joe Girard. Director was Scott Pembroke.

WINDS OF THE WASTELAND 1936 (Republic). The cast included Phyllis Fraser, Yakima Canutt and Lane Chandler. Director was Mack V. Wright.

THE SEA SPOILERS 1936 (Universal). The cast included Nan Grey, William Bakewell and Russell Hicks. Director was Frank Strayer.

THE LONELY TRAIL 1936 (Republic). The cast included Ann Rutherford, Cy Kendall, Sam Flint and Yakima Canutt. Director was Joseph Kane.

CONFLICT 1936 (Universal). The cast included Jean Rogers, Tommy Bupp and Ward Bond. Director was David Howard.

CALIFORNIA STRAIGHT AHEAD 1937 (Universal). The cast included Louise Latimer, Robert McWade and Tully Marshall. Director was Arthur Lubin.

I COVER THE WAR 1937 (Universal). The cast included Gwen Gaze, James Bush and Pat Somerset. Director was Arthur Lubin.

IDOL OF THE CROWDS 1937 (Universal). The cast included Sheila Bromley, Billy Burrud and Russell Gordon. Director was Arthur Lubin.

ADVENTURE'S END 1937 (Universal). The cast included Diana Gibson, Montagu Love, Ben Carter and Glenn Strange. Director was Arthur Lubin.

BORN TO THE WEST 1937 (Paramount). The cast included Marsha Hunt, John Mack Brown, James Craig and Monte Blue. Director was Charles Barton.

PALS OF THE SADDLE 1938 (Republic). The cast included Ray Corrigan, Max Terhune and Doreen McKay. Director was George Sherman.

OVERLAND STAGE RAIDERS 1938 (Republic). The cast included Ray Corrigan, Louise Brooks, Fern Emmett and Frank LaRue. Director was George Sherman.

SANTA FE STAMPEDE 1938 (Republic). The cast included June Martel, Max Terhune and William Farnum. Director was George Sherman.

RED RIVER RANGE 1938 (Republic). The cast included Ray Corrigan, Max Terhune and Polly Moran. Director was George Sherman.

STAGECOACH 1939 (United Artists). The cast included Claire Trevor, Andy Devine and George Bancroft. Director was John Ford.

THE NIGHT RIDERS 1939 (Republic). The cast included Ray Corrigan, Doreen McKay, Ruth Rogers and Tom Tyler. Director was George Sherman.

THREE TEXAS STEERS 1939 (Republic). The cast included Carole Landis, Max Terhune and Ralph Graves. Director was George Sherman.

WYOMING OUTLAW 1939 (Republic). The cast included Adele Pearce, Raymond Hatton, Donald Barry and Yakima Canutt. Director was George Sherman.

NEW FRONTIER 1939 (Republic). The cast included Ray Corrigan, Phyllis Isley and Dave O'Brien. Director was George Sherman.

ALLEGHENY UPRISING 1939 (RKO). The cast included Claire Trevor, George Sanders and Robert Barrat. Director was William Seiter.

DARK COMMAND 1940 (Republic). The cast included Walter Pidgeon, Roy Rogers and Claire Trevor. Director was Raoul Walsh.

THREE FACES WEST 1940 (Republic). The cast included Sigrid Gurie, Charles Coburn and Trevor Bardette. Director was Bernard Vorhaus.

THE LONG VOYAGE HOME 1940 (United Artists). The cast included Thomas Mitchell, Mildred Natwick, Ward Bond and Arthur Shields. Director was John Ford.

SEVEN SINNERS 1940 (Universal). The cast included Marlene Dietrich, Broderick Crawford and Anna Lee. Director was Tay Garnett.

A MAN BETRAYED 1941 (Republic). The cast included Frances Dee, Wallace Ford, Ward Bond and Tim Ryan. Director was John H. Auer.

LADY FROM LOUISIANA 1941 (Republic). The cast included Ona Munson, Ray Middleton, Helen Westley and Dorothy Dandridge. Director was Bernard Vorhaus.

THE SHEPHERD OF THE HILLS 1941 (Paramount). The cast included Betty Field, Harry Carey, James Barton and Ward Bond. Director was Henry Hathaway.

LADY FOR A NIGHT 1941 (Republic). The cast included Joan Blondell, Ray Middleton and Philip Merivale. Director was Leigh Jason.

REAP THE WILD WIND 1942 (Paramount). The cast included Ray Milland, Paulette Goddard, Raymond Massey and Susan Hayward. Director was Cecil B. DeMille.

THE SPOILERS 1942 (Universal). The cast included Marlene Dietrich, Randolph Scott, Margaret Lindsay and Harry Carey. Director was Ray Enright.

IN OLD CALIFORNIA 1942 (Republic). The cast included Helen Parrish, Patsy Kelly, Edgar Kennedy and Dick Purcell. Director was William McGann.

FLYING TIGERS 1942 (Republic). The cast included Anna Lee, Paul Kelly, Gordon Jones and Mae Clarke. Director was David Miller.

"Stagecoach" (1939). Wayne at far right.

REUNION IN FRANCE 1942 (MGM). The cast included Joan Crawford, Reginald Owen and John Carradine. Director was Jules Dassin.

PITTSBURGH 1942 (Universal). The cast included Marlene Dietrich and Randolph Scott. Director was Lewis Seiler.

A LADY TAKES A CHANCE 1943 (RKO). The cast included Jean Arthur, Phil Silvers and Don Costello. The cast included William A. Seiter.

IN OLD OKLAHOMA 1943 (Republic). The cast included Dale Evans, George Hayes and Paul Fix. Director was Albert S. Rogell.

THE FIGHTING SEABEES 1944 (Republic). The cast included Susan Hayward, William Frawley and George Hayes. Directors were Howard Lydecker and Edward Ludwig.

TALL IN THE SADDLE 1944 (RKO). The cast included Ella Raines, Ward Bond and George Hayes. Director was Edwin Marin.

FLAME OF THE BARBARY COAST 1945 (Republic). The cast included Ann Dvorak, William Frawley and Virginia Grey. Director was Joseph Kane.

BACK TO BATAAN 1945 (RKO). The cast included Anthony Quinn and Richard Loo. Director was Edward Dmytryk.

DAKOTA 1945 (Republic). The cast included Vera Ralston, Walter Brennan and Ward Bond. Director was Joseph Kane.

THEY WERE EXPENDABLE 1945 (MGM). The cast included Donna Reed, Robert Montgomery and Jack Holt. Director was John Ford.

WITHOUT RESERVATIONS 1946 (RKO). The cast included Claudette Colbert, Don DeFore and Phil Brown. Director was Mervyn LeRoy.

ANGEL AND THE BADMAN 1947 (Republic). The cast included Gail Russell, Bruce Cabot and Irene Rich. Director was James Edward Grant.

TYCOON 1947 (RKO). The cast included Sir Cedric Hardwicke, Anthony Quinn and Paul Fix. Director was Richard Wallace.

FORT APACHE 1948 (RKO). The cast included Henry Fonda and Shirley Temple. Director was John Ford.

RED RIVER 1948 (United Artists). The cast included Montgomery Clift, Walter Brennan and Joanne Dru. Director was Howard Hawks.

THREE GODFATHERS 1948 (MGM). The cast included Pedro Armendariz and Harry Carey, Jr. Director was John Ford.

WAKE OF THE RED WITCH 1948 (Republic). The cast included Gail Russell and Gig Young. Director was Edward Ludwig.

SHE WORE A YELLOW RIBBON 1949 (RKO). The cast included Joanne Dru, Ben Johnson and Victor McLaglen. Director was John Ford.

THE FIGHTING KENTUCKIAN 1949 (Republic). The cast included Vera Ralston, Philip Dorn and Paul Fix. Director was George Waggner.

SANDS OF IWO JIMA 1949 (Republic). The cast included Forrest Tucker, James Brown and Richard Webb. Director was Allan Dwan.

RIO GRANDE 1950 (Republic) The cast included Maureen O'Hara, Ben Johnson and Chill Wills. Director was John Ford.

OPERATION PACIFIC 1951 (Warner Brothers). The cast included Patricia Neal and Ward Bond. Director was George Waggner.

FLYING LEATHERNECKS 1951 (RKO). The cast included Robert Ryan and Janis Carter. Director was Nicholas Ray.

THE QUIET MAN 1952 (Republic). The cast included Maureen O'Hara and three of Wayne's children, Patrick, Michael and Melinda. Director was John Ford.

BIG JIM McLAIN 1952 (Warner Brothers). The cast included James Arness and Nancy Olson. Director was Edward Ludwig.

TROUBLE ALONG THE WAY 1953 (Warner Brothers). The cast included Donna Reed and Charles Coburn. Director was Michael Curtiz.

ISLAND IN THE SKY 1953 (Warner Brothers). The cast included Lloyd Nolan, James Arness and Andy Devine. Director was William A. Wellman.

HONDO 1953 (Warner Brothers). The cast included Geraldine Page, James Arness and Ward Bond. Director was John Farrow.

THE HIGH AND THE MIGHTY 1954 (Warner Brothers). The cast included Claire Trevor, Robert Stack and Phil Harris. Director was William A. Wellman.

With Vera Ralston in "Dakota" (1945).

"She Wore a Yellow Ribbon" (1949).

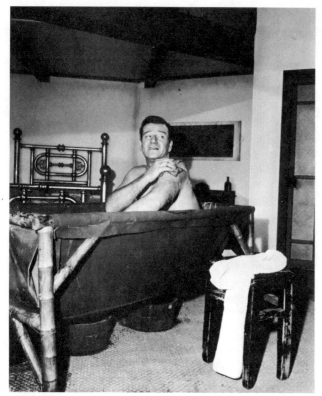

"Blood Alley" (1955).

With Janet Leigh in "Jet Pilot" (1957).

THE SEA CHASE 1955 (Warner Brothers). The cast included Lana Turner, Tab Hunter and James Arness. Director was John Farrow.

BLOOD ALLEY 1955 (Warner Brothers). The cast included Lauren Bacall and Anita Ekberg. Director was William A. Wellman.

THE CONQUEROR 1956 (RKO). The cast included Susan Hayward, Agnes Moorehead and William Conrad. Director was Dick Powell.

THE SEARCHERS 1956 (Warner Brothers). The cast included Vera Miles, Natalie Wood. Director was John Ford.

THE WINGS OF EAGLES 1957 (MGM). The cast included Dan Dailey, Maureen O'Hara and Ward Bond. Director was John Ford.

JET PILOT 1957 (RKO). The cast included Janet Leigh and Hans Conreid. Director was Josef von Sternberg.

LEGEND OF THE LOST 1957 (United Artists). The cast included Sophia Loren and Rossano Brazzi. Director was Henry Hathaway.

I MARRIED A WOMAN 1958 (RKO). The cast included George Gobel and Diana Dors. Director was Hal Kanter.

THE BARBARIAN AND THE GEISHA 1958 (Twentieth Century-Fox). The cast included Eiko Ando and Sam Jaffe. Director was John Huston.

RIO BRAVO 1959 (Warner Brothers). The cast included Dean Martin, Ricky Nelson, Angie Dickinson and Walter Brennan. Director was Howard Hawks.

THE HORSE SOLDIERS 1959 (United Artists). The cast included William Holden and Constance Towers. Director was John Ford.

THE ALAMO 1960 (United Artists). The cast included Richard Widmark, Laurence Harvey, Richard Boone, Frankie Avalon and Linda Cristal. Director was John Wayne.

NORTH TO ALASKA 1960 (Twentieth Century-Fox). The cast included Stewart Granger, Ernie Kovacs, Fabian and Capucine. Director was Henry Hathaway.

THE COMANCHEROS 1961 (Twentieth Century-Fox). The cast included Stuart Whitman and Lee Marvin. Director was Michael Curtiz.

THE MAN WHO SHOT LIBERTY VALANCE 1962 (Paramount). The cast included James Stewart, Vera Miles, Lee Marvin and Andy Devine. Director was John Ford.

Wayne paddles an outraged Maureen O'Hara in "McLintock!" (1963).

HATARI 1962 (Paramount). The cast included Red Buttons and Elsa Martinelli. Director was Howard Hawks.

THE LONGEST DAY 1962 (Twentieth Century-Fox). The cast included Robert Mitchum, Henry Fonda, Robert Ryan, Rod Steiger and Richard Burton. Director was Ken Annakin.

HOW THE WEST WAS WON 1962 (MGM). The cast included Lee J. Cobb, Henry Fonda and Karl Malden. Directors were Henry Hathaway, John Ford and George Marshall.

DONOVAN'S REEF 1963 (Paramount). The cast included Lee Marvin, Cesar Romero and Dorothy Lamour. Director was John Ford.

McLINTOCK! 1963 (United Artists). The cast included Maureen O'Hara, Yvonne DeCarlo and Edgar Buchanan. Director was Andrew V. McLaglen.

CIRCUS WORLD 1964 (Paramount). The cast included Rita Hayworth and Claudia Cardinale. Director was Henry Hathaway.

THE GREATEST STORY EVER TOLD 1965 (United Artists). The cast included Max Von Sydow, Dorothy McGuire and Charlton Heston. Director was George Stevens.

IN HARM'S WAY 1965 (Paramount). The cast included Kirk Douglas, Patricia Neal. Director was Otto Preminger.

THE SONS OF KATIE ELDER 1965 (Paramount). The cast included Dean Martin and George Kennedy. Director was Henry Hathaway.

CAST A GIANT SHADOW 1966 (United Artists). The cast included Kirk Douglas, Yul Brynner, Angie Dickinson. Director was Melville Shavelson.

THE WAR WAGON 1967 (Universal). The cast included Kirk Douglas and Robert Walker. Director was Burt Kennedy.

EL DORADO 1967 (Paramount). The cast included Robert Mitchum and Edward Asner. Director was Howard Hawks.

THE GREEN BERETS 1968 (Warner Brothers). The cast included David Janssen, Jim Hutton and Aldo Ray. Directors were John Wayne and Ray Kellogg.

HELLFIGHTERS 1968 (Universal). The cast included Vera Miles and Katherine Ross. Director was Andrew McLaglen.

TRUE GRIT 1969 (Paramount). The cast included Glen Campbell and Kim Darby. Director was Henry Hathaway.

THE UNDEFEATED 1969 (Twentieth Century-Fox). The cast included Rock Hudson and Roman Gabriel. Director was Andrew McLaglen.

CHISUM 1970 (Warner Brothers). The cast included Glenn Corbett and Forrest Tucker. Director was Andrew McLaglen.

RIO LOBO 1970 (National General). The cast included Jennifer O'Neill and George Plimpton. Director was Howard Hawks.

BIG JAKE 1971 (National General). The cast included Richard Boone, Maureen O'Hara and Bobby Vinton. Director was George Sherman.

As Rooster Cogburn in "True Grit" (1969), a performance which earned Wayne an "Oscar."

THE COWBOYS 1972 (Warner Brothers). The cast included Colleen Dewhurst and Bruce Dern. Director was Mark Rydell.

THE TRAIN ROBBERS 1973 (Warner Brothers). The cast included Ann-Margaret, Christopher George and Ricardo Montalban. Director was Burt Kennedy.

CAHILL 1973 (Warner Brothers). The cast included Gary Grimes and Neville Brand. Director was Andrew McLaglen.

McQ 1974 (Warner Brothers). The cast included Eddie Albert, Diana Muldaur, Julie Adams and Colleen Dewhurst. Director was John Sturges.

ROOSTER COGBURN 1975 (Universal). The cast included Katherine Hepburn, Anthony Zerbe, John McIntire and Strother Martin. Director was Stuart Millar.

THE SHOOTIST 1976 (Paramount). The cast included Lauren Bacall, James Stewart and Ron Howard. Director was Don Siegel.

"The Shootist" (1976), The "Duke's" last film.